I. M. Pei

by Mary Englar

Raintree

Chicago, Illinois

© 2006 Raintree
Published by Raintree, a division of Reed Elsevier, Inc.
Chicago, Illinois
Customer Service: 888-363-4266
Visit our website at www.raintreelibrary.com

Printed and bound in the United States at Lake Book Manufacturing, Inc.
10 09 08 07 06
10 9 8 7 6 5 4 3

Library of Congress Cataloging-in-Publication Data:
Englar, Mary.
  I. M. Pei / Mary Englar.-- 1st ed.
    p. cm. -- (Asian-American biographies)
  Includes bibliographical references and index.
  ISBN 1-4109-1056-3 (hc) -- ISBN 1-4109-1129-2 (pb)
  1. Pei, I. M., 1917---Juvenile literature. 2. Chinese American architects--Biography--Juvenile literature. I. Pei, I. M., 1917- II. Title.
III. Series.
  NA737.P365E54 2005
  720'.92--dc22
                        2005005638

Acknowledgments
The publisher would like to thank the following for permission to reproduce photographs:
AP p. 54 (Wide World Photos); Corbis pp. 4 (Owen Franken), 6 (Katy Winn), 14 (Kevin Fleming), 30 (Bettmann), 35 (Adam Woolfitt), 36 (Wally McNamee), 37 (Bettmann), 38 (Charles & Josette Lenars), 41 (Owen Franken), 42 (Bettmann), 44 (Reed Kaestner), 51 (Robert Holmes), 52 (Owen Franken), 53 (Free Agents Limited), 59 (Bettmann); Getty Images pp. 8 (Hulton Archive/Topical Press Agency), 12 (Photodisc), 17 (Hulton Archive), 21 (Hulton Archive), 22 (Time Life Pictures), 25 (Time Life Pictures/Ralph Morse), 29 (Time Life Pictures), 49 (Agence France-Presse/Frank Perry); Kerun Ip p. 57; Magnum Photos p. 46 (Harry Gruyaert); MAP p. 10; Photohome p. 27 (Allen Matheson); The Image Works p. 34 (Margot Granitsas).

Cover photograph: The Image Works (David Lassman/Syracuse Newspapers)

Some words are shown in bold, **like this**. You can find out what they mean by looking in the glossary.

Contents

I.M. Pei. stands in front of the pyramid entrance he designed at the Louvre Museum in Paris, France.

Introduction

Ieoh Ming Pei (pronounced "pay") is one of the most famous American **architects** in the world. Two of his most famous **designs** are the Rock and Roll Hall of Fame and Museum in Cleveland, Ohio, and a new entrance for the Louvre Museum in Paris, France. I. M. Pei believes that how people use the building is one of the most important parts of architecture. His design for a bank might provide space for the workers to enjoy a garden. His museums invite visitors to enjoy the art from different points of view.

Pei came to the United States from China to study architecture in 1935. Because World War II was being fought (1939–1945), Pei's father encouraged him to stay in the United States. In 1978 the Chinese government invited Pei to return to China. He accepted a project for a new hotel near Beijing. Pei believed the Chinese should use their own **traditions** to start a new **style** of Chinese architecture.

Pei is pictured here with his grandson Matthew in 2004.

However, for most of his career, Pei **designed** buildings in a modern **style**. He used shapes, such as triangles, rectangles, and **pyramids,** to create new buildings that looked nothing like the old **architecture** in the United States and Europe. He also wanted people to feel comfortable as they moved around inside his buildings and to be surprised by details or views.

I. M. Pei has spent his entire life designing museums, **skyscrapers**, and office towers. He received every major award for architecture. Even after he officially retired in 1990, he spent time designing small projects so he could work on the details of his architectural style. With more than 50 buildings all over the world, Pei has created many buildings for people to enjoy.

In His Own Words

"I like to think that buildings are designed for people. For that reason I prefer to design public buildings which are used by a lot of people."

"You have to say to yourself, 'If I believe something is right, it doesn't matter who I am.' Take your position and have faith in yourself."

This picture shows Hong Kong in the early twentieth century.

Chapter 1:
Growing Up in China

Ieoh Ming Pei was born April 26, 1917, in Guangzhou, China. His father, Tsuyee, worked for the Bank of China. Ieoh Ming's mother, Lien Kwun, stayed at home and took care of Ieoh Ming and his older sister, Yuen Hua. When Ieoh Ming was born, many conflicts were tearing China apart. In 1918 Ieoh Ming's father decided to take his family to Hong Kong for safety. Hong Kong was a British **colony**, and the British army protected it.

In the early 1900s, many Chinese people wanted a new kind of government. For hundreds of years, an emperor had ruled China. The emperor allowed other countries to control trade and take over Chinese land. Great Britain, Russia, Japan, and France all controlled parts of China. The Chinese people wanted to make decisions about their own country. They **rebelled** against the emperor.

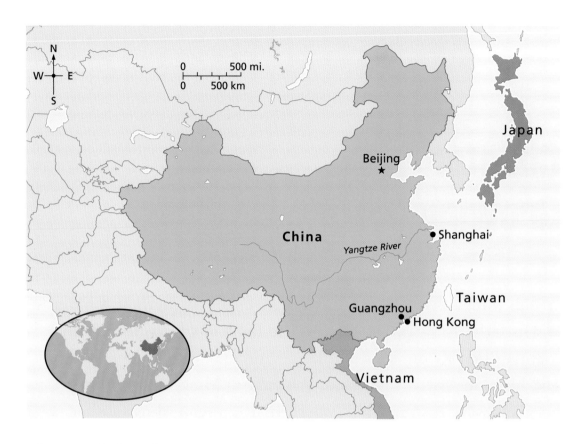

This map of China shows some of the cities where Ieoh Ming lived and worked.

In 1912, the last Chinese emperor agreed to give up his throne. The new government was called the Republic of China. But the new government did not have strong rulers, and many Chinese people disagreed about how the government should work. When Ieoh Ming was born, **warlords** controlled much of the Chinese countryside. The warlords forced the Chinese people to give them money and food. The Pei family moved to Hong Kong to get away from the warlords.

Ieoh Ming's Family Moves to Shanghai

Ieoh Ming's family stayed in Hong Kong for about ten years. One younger sister and two younger brothers were born in Hong Kong. In 1927 the family moved to Shanghai. Shanghai is a port city at the mouth of the Yangtze River in China. The Yangtze is the longest river in China. Many products, such as rubber, cotton, coal, and silk were shipped along the river.

Shanghai was growing when Ieoh Ming and his family arrived. Many Europeans lived there and traded products with the Chinese. They built houses and office buildings in the European **style**. The main road along the waterfront was lined with European **architecture**.

Ieoh Ming's father, Tsuyee Pei, was promoted to manager at the Shanghai branch of the Bank of China. He moved his family into a two-story house with a large backyard in a European neighborhood. Tsuyee Pei had a good job and traveled often. Ieoh Ming respected his father, but he did not get to know him very well.

In contrast Ieoh Ming was very close to his mother, Lien Kwun. She played the flute and wrote poetry, and taught her children about Chinese **traditions**. Ieoh Ming knew he could ask his mother for advice about life or school. Lien Kwun became very sick and died when Ieoh Ming was 13. As the oldest son, he was expected to be strong for his other siblings.

As a boy, Ieoh Ming spent many summers with his grandfather in Suzhou. Suzhou is famous for its gardens.

Summers in Suzhou

The Pei family came from the ancient city of Suzhou, which is not far from Shanghai. Ieoh Ming's grandfather still lived in Suzhou when Ieoh Ming was young, so Ieoh Ming often spent time there in the summers with his grandfather and cousins. Ieoh Ming's grandfather taught Ieoh Ming about **traditional** Chinese values. He learned to obey his parents, to never show anger, and to speak clearly at all times.

School Days

Ieoh Ming attended an American **missionary** school in Shanghai. Most students lived at the school and wore uniforms. Although most classes were taught in Chinese, Ieoh Ming also learned English. Ieoh Ming was an excellent student. He studied hard, but he also liked to play tennis and volleyball. Ieoh Ming also liked American movies. The Americans seemed happy in the movies. Ieoh Ming thought the United States looked like a good place to go to college.

Planning His Future

Ieoh Ming and his father discussed his future as he got older. His father wanted Ieoh Ming to study overseas to become a banker or a doctor. Ieoh Ming did not know what he wanted to be. Ieoh Ming went to his school's library to read about colleges in Europe and the United States. He decided he wanted to study in the United States or France. Pei's father suggested Ieoh Ming apply to Oxford University in England. Ieoh Ming passed the entrance exams for Oxford, but he asked his father to let him study in the United States.

In 1934, Ieoh Ming watched a new hotel get built near to his favorite movie theater in Shanghai. Before the project started, the tallest building in Shanghai was eight stories tall. The Park Hotel would be 26 stories. Pei watched as the construction workers added floor after floor. For him building a **skyscraper** seemed as exciting as going to the Moon. He returned to the school library. The description of **architecture** courses came close to what he wanted to learn about.

Pei first chose to study architecture at Massachusetts Institute of Technology.

Chapter 2:
Studying Architecture in the United States

In August 1935, Pei boarded a ship for San Francisco, California, with a friend from school. They were both going to the University of Pennsylvania in Philadelphia. After a couple of days of sightseeing, Pei and his friend took a train to Philadelphia. It was a good way to see the country. Pei worried that his English was not very good, but he was excited to see the country he knew only from the movies.

The **architecture** program in Philadelphia was very different from what Pei expected. He was very good at math and science, but the program expected students to draw copies of famous European buildings. Beautiful drawings and paintings made by his classmates covered the hallways outside their classrooms. Pei did not know how to draw. He was afraid he had made a big mistake.

Two weeks after Pei started classes, some Chinese friends came to visit from the Massachusetts Institute of Technology (MIT) near Boston, Massachusetts. They loved MIT and encouraged Pei to transfer. Pei knew he did not want to learn to draw. He decided that if **architecture** required him to draw, he would be better at **engineering**. After talking to his friends, he applied to the School of Engineering at MIT.

Massachusetts Institute of Technology

Pei was much happier at MIT. He liked Boston, and there were more than 70 Chinese students at MIT. He settled in to study engineering. Not long after he arrived, his teachers noticed that he had a talent for **design**.

The head of MIT's School of Architecture, William Emerson, took an interest in Pei and his career. He took him on walking tours around Boston and showed him the different **styles** of the buildings. Emerson told Pei he had a talent for design. Pei decided to transfer to the architecture program.

A New Style of Architecture

Pei learned to draw the old design styles with his classmates. But he thought there must be a better way to design. He wanted to look to the future rather than the past. He spent hours in the library looking at architecture books. Some architects in Europe had begun to design a new kind of building. They were creating

This picture shows Boston Public Gardens in the early 1930s. Pei was studying in Boston at this time.

buildings that were plain on the outside, but more comfortable for people than the great cathedrals and palaces of Europe.

Pei's teachers at MIT did not teach the new style that became known as **modern architecture**. He learned everything he could from books. The new architecture used steel, cement, and glass, and did not have any decoration. In the United States, Frank Lloyd Wright had created a new style as well. His houses and buildings were built into the land. Wright used walls of windows and skylights to bring nature indoors. Pei visited some of Wright's buildings, but he preferred the modern work of the Europeans.

Pei Meets His Future Wife

In 1938 Pei visited New York City to see a friend. His friend introduced him to a young Chinese woman named Eileen Loo. She was on her way to study at Wellesley College, a women's college near Boston. After he met Eileen, he called to ask her on a date. They had many things in common. Eileen was interested in **design** and **engineering**. Pei eventually asked Eileen to marry him, but she wanted to finish school. In June 1942, five days after she graduated, they were married.

War Interrupts Pei's Return to China

Both Pei and Eileen planned to return to China to live after they finished college. When Pei graduated in 1940, China was at war with Japan. Pei's father told him he should stay in the United States. By the time Eileen graduated in 1942, the United States was at war with Japan and Germany. World War II started in 1939 when Germany invaded Poland in Europe. The United States stayed out of the war until the Japanese bombed Pearl Harbor in Hawaii on December 7, 1941.

Pei hoped that the United States and its **allies** would defeat the Japanese. He wanted the Japanese to leave China. He still planned to live in China when the war ended. Eileen planned to study landscape **architecture** at Harvard. Landscape architects design the land around buildings in a way that is good for people and the environment.

Studying At Harvard

Pei decided to continue his studies at Harvard as well. He enrolled in a master's of architecture program in December 1942. One of the reasons Pei chose Harvard was the department taught the modern **style** of architecture. The professors had come from Europe to escape World War II. They believed that **modern architecture** could provide better buildings for more people.

Pei listened carefully to his professors. He liked the idea of a new style. He also wondered how simple squares and straight lines would fit in at home in China. He wanted to use some of the techniques that modern architects used. But he also wanted to study the people, the **culture**, and the land when he designed a new building.

For his master's project, Pei designed a modern museum that might be built in Shanghai. Pei planned **displays** for small glass vases, jade carvings, and small paintings. Each room of the museum looked out on a garden. In the center, visitors looked through glass walls at a large garden. A stream ran through the garden and the trees and flowers were carefully planned. Pei's professors liked his work and encouraged him to look for ways to include his Chinese culture in his designs.

Two Children and Graduation

Pei and Eileen had their first son in 1945. They named him T'ing Chung. Eileen stayed home to take care of the new baby. In 1946 they had another son, Chien Chung. They did not teach their children Chinese. They still hoped to return to live in China, where the children could learn Chinese easily.

Pei graduated from Harvard with a master's degree in **architecture** in 1946. He wrote to his father about coming home. Once again his father advised him to stay in the United States a bit longer. After the end of World War II, the Japanese left China. The war had destroyed farmland, businesses, and the economy. Pei's father told him it would be a bad time to come home. Pei accepted a part-time teaching job at Harvard.

The Communist Revolution in China

At the end of World War II in 1945, the Nationalist government of China tried to rebuild the country. Chiang Kai-shek led the Nationalist Government. The government charged the Chinese people many taxes to help rebuild railroads, roads, and cities. When people could not pay the taxes, the government took their crops instead. The Chinese people were starving, and there were no jobs and no way to make money.

Soon a **civil war** broke out between the Nationalist government and a group called the Chinese **Communist** Party led by Mao

Zedong. From 1945 until 1949, the two groups fought over who would rule China. The Nationalists controlled the cities, but the Communists controlled the countryside where 80 percent of the Chinese people lived. Mao promised to make changes that would allow everyone to have a job and enough food to eat. Most important he promised peace. After years of war, the Chinese people wanted peace.

In 1949 the Communists took Beijing and drove the Nationalists out of China. Chiang and his followers retreated to the island of Taiwan, 100 miles (160 kilometers) from the coast of China. Mao founded the People's Republic of China in October 1949. He ruled China as the leader of the Chinese Communist Party for 27 years.

The revolution brought many good changes to China. For the first time, all Chinese people could get an education, and everyone had a job. At first workers were paid with food, so most had enough to eat. But the revolution also brought some problems. The Chinese people were not allowed to speak out against the new government. When this happened many Chinese who were living in the United States became afraid to go home.

William Zeckendorf, a New York City real estate developer, offered Pei his first job.

Chapter 3:
First Jobs

For two years Pei taught classes in **architecture** to small groups of students at Harvard. He enjoyed teaching the students how to draw what was in their imaginations. He felt he learned more about architecture as a teacher than he did as a student.

A New Job in Real Estate

Most new architects start with small jobs, such as **designing** new houses. Pei wanted to design large buildings, **skyscrapers**, and even entire neighborhoods. He knew that the money he earned from small projects would not support his growing family. In 1948 William Zeckendorf invited Pei to New York City for a job interview. Zeckendorf owned a large **real estate** company called Webb & Knapp. His company planned hotels, new housing, and office buildings in New York City.

Pei liked Zeckendorf immediately. Zeckendorf had big ideas to completely change the buildings and neighborhoods of major cities. He offered Pei a job as Webb & Knapp's director of architectural research. Pei took some time to think about the job offer. Most architects did not work for **real estate** companies. The real estate companies usually hired architects for single projects. This job was not a **traditional** career choice for an architect.

Working on Big Projects

But Pei also wanted to learn about how large projects were **developed** in the United States. Zeckendorf bought large areas of land in a city, and then built new housing and businesses. Zeckendorf's job offered practical experience in **designing** big projects that included many different kinds of buildings. Pei accepted the job and moved to New York City.

His first assignment was to redo Webb & Knapp's offices. Pei started with the front office. When customers came in, they looked through large windows at an outdoor terrace. An elegant statue and twisted pine trees surrounded a pool of water. He placed Zeckendorf's office right in the middle of the room. A steel elevator rose one floor to a circular dining room on the roof. Everyone liked the new offices. Pei was off to a good start.

Pei's first assignment was to redesign Webb & Knapp's offices.

Growing Success

In the 1950s Zeckendorf and Pei flew around the country to talk to city planners about new projects. They met mayors and toured the land to be **developed**. Then Zeckendorf told the planners what they needed to make the city more modern. Pei listened to how Zeckendorf persuaded people. Pei learned how to convince mayors and bankers that new buildings brought more people into the cities. Soon Pei's confidence and enthusiasm helped bring new business to Webb & Knapp.

Mile High Center in Denver, Colorado

The first major building that Pei **designed** for Zeckendorf was a 23-story office tower in downtown Denver, Colorado. Much of Denver had old, brick buildings. When Mile High Center was finished in 1956, many people in Denver called it a **skyscraper**. The office tower was a plain rectangle. But Pei made it look unusual by using different materials to create a woven texture.

Pei used features for Mile High Center that he continued to use throughout his career. He set the building back from the street and put it up on stilts. This allowed people to move under the building to the open **plaza** behind it. Pei placed many flowerbeds and trees around a trout pond. The plaza gave office workers a nice place to sit and enjoy the sun.

Mile High Center quickly filled with new businesses. The plaza was a new idea and attracted many people. For the first time, Pei became well known to other architects and builders. As the director of **architecture**, Pei supervised a team of many architects. He created the original design, but then his workers carried out the everyday details of large projects. But Pei always checked the plans to see if he could make them better.

The Mile High Center was the tallest building in Denver when it was first built.

A Weekend House in the Country

In 1950 Pei and Eileen had another son, Sandi. The growing family still lived in a small apartment in New York City. Pei decided they needed a place to get away on weekends. In 1952 he **designed** a simple house to be built in the hills of Katonah, New York. The house was built on a hill and looked out over the woods. Pei planted Chinese evergreen trees around the house to remind him of home.

The frame for the house went up in one day. Pei and a friend spent another day putting in the screens for the large porch. The square floor was raised on stilts, and the rooms were open and filled with light. Pei put rollers on his children's beds so they could push them out and sleep on the porch on warm nights.

Pei and Eileen Become American Citizens

Pei and Eileen had always hoped to return to China. They felt comfortable in the United States, but they missed China. After the Chinese **civil war** ended in 1949, Pei's father Tsuyee returned to Shanghai. But the new government was very different from the old one. Tsuyee soon moved to Hong Kong, and finally came to New York City.

By 1955, Pei knew that he and Eileen would not return to China to live and work. He and Eileen studied to take the citizenship test to become Americans. Pei and Eileen took the oath of citizenship at New York City's Polo Grounds. Ten thousand new citizens recited the oath together on November 11, 1955.

In 1955, Pei took an oath of citizenship with 10,000 other immigrants in New York City.

Pei stopped for a photograph taken at his own architecture business in 1967.

Chapter 4:
Pei Starts His Own Company

During his years with Zeckendorf, Pei worked long hours to find new customers, plan projects, and manage about 70 employees. In 1955, he decided to start his own company called I. M. Pei & Associates. If he stayed with Zeckendorf, Pei believed he would never **design** anything but office towers and housing projects. He wanted to design museums and concert halls, too.

In 1960, Pei finally stopped working for Zeckendorf. Most of his team of **architects** stayed with him. He felt free to look for new projects. But he also worried whether he could bring in enough business to keep his team busy.

National Center for Atmospheric Research in Boulder, Colorado

In the fall of 1961, Pei was chosen to **design** a new scientific laboratory in the mountains above Boulder, Colorado. For the first time in many years, he had the time to design a project and follow all the details until it was finished. He felt like an **architect** again.

Walter Roberts was the new director for the university committee for atmospheric research. This organization of scientists studied changes in the atmosphere and the causes of acid rain. Roberts wanted the new building to encourage the scientists to work together. The location in the mountains allowed the scientists to study nature outside, too.

Pei studied the location for several months. The mountains behind the building **site** were huge. He knew his building could not compete with nature. He studied ancient Pueblo Indian homes. He liked the way the buildings blended into the side of the cliffs. Pei wanted the new center to blend into the mountains.

Roberts rejected several designs. Finally, they both agreed on one. The building would be made of concrete. They needed a strong material to stand up to the cold, snow, and wind of Colorado winters. Pei set the building at the foot of a cliff. He mixed concrete with sand from the mountain to get a color that blended with the cliffs. The final building allowed scientists to meet on winding staircases and outdoor patios. It was a great success.

John F. Kennedy Library in Boston, Massachusetts

In 1964, the year after the death of President John F. Kennedy, Mrs. Kennedy started a search for an architect to design his presidential library. Many architects around the world wanted to work on this project. After a long process, Mrs. Kennedy picked Pei for the job. Though Pei was not well known, she liked his modern **style** and that he planned his designs to fit the landscape.

President Kennedy had wanted his library to be built in Boston in the area where he had grown up. Harvard University had already offered a site, and Pei began to plan. Soon after he started, he realized that there was not enough land for the project. Another location was chosen, but the people who lived nearby thought it could cause problems for the neighborhood. One hold up after another tested Pei's patience.

In the end it took thirteen years to finish the project. The library was built at the edge of Boston Harbor. The design changed many times as Pei tried to please everyone. The building ended up smaller and less detailed than Pei's early plan. Pei was unhappy with the final design, but many visitors admired the library that opened in 1979.

Pei designed skylights to flood the lobby of the East Building with natural light.

East Building of the National Gallery of Art in Washington, D.C.

When Pei was chosen to work on the Kennedy Library, he became well known all over the world. His company grew and took on more and more projects. In 1968 Pei was offered a difficult challenge in Washington, D.C. The National Gallery of Art on the Capitol Mall needed more space for art and for storage. Pei was chosen to build a new East Building.

Pei used triangles to make the East Building fit into a small space.

The land for the new museum was an odd shape. It was not a rectangle like most building **sites**. Pei tried many **designs** before he found one that used triangles to make the best use of the site. Between the triangle-shaped buildings, Pei designed a **courtyard** with a glass roof. When visitors entered the courtyard, they could look up several stories to an unusual ceiling that let sunlight into the room. In Pei's usual **style**, he created a space for visitors to meet and then move off to different rooms of the museum.

Pei celebrates at the opening ceremony of the East Building of the National Gallery of Art in Washington, D.C.

It was very important for Pei to make his building blend in on the Capitol Mall. The buildings on the Mall were mostly **traditional styles**. The National Gallery of Art was built with marble from Tennessee. Pei used the same pink marble for the outside walls of the new building. The walls blend in with the monuments that surround it very well. But, the sharp, modern style is unique on the Mall.

Pei worked with government officials to make his buildings fit with their locations.

When the East Building opened in 1978, over a million people visited in the first two months. Hundreds of children who visited the museum wrote to Pei telling him how much they liked it. Pei became known as one of the best **modern architects** in the United States.

This picture shows Tiananmen Square, Beijing, in the mid-1970s.

Chapter 5:
Return to China

In 1974, Pei returned to China for the first time. He traveled around the country with a group of **architects**. Though he did not like the new architecture he saw there, he was happy to see that most Chinese people had good clothes and enough to eat. Compared to the war and hunger he left in 1937, the new government had improved the lives of its people.

Fragrant Hill Hotel Near Beijing

In 1978 the Chinese government invited Pei to come to China and give a speech about architecture. The Chinese wanted to build taller buildings to house their growing population and the many tourists who visited China. Pei spoke against **skyscrapers**. He asked the Chinese to remember their **traditions**. He was afraid that skyscrapers near an area called the **Forbidden City** in the center of Beijing would detract from the beautiful palace there. In the past, Chinese emperors had lived in the Forbidden City.

Only the emperor and his family were allowed inside the palace gates, so it became known as the **Forbidden City**.

The Chinese were eager to have Pei build something, even if it was not a **skyscraper**. They invited him to return in December 1978. He told them he was spending Christmas with his family. The Chinese invited him to bring his family, too. So, Pei, Eileen, their four children, and two grandchildren traveled to China. His children met many of their relatives for the first time.

Government officials took Pei to several possible **sites**. About 25 miles (40 kilometers) outside of Beijing, he toured a forest that Chinese emperors had used for hunting. It was called Fragrant Hill. Pei liked it immediately. In December the trees and steep hills were covered with snow. Pei imagined a building that fit at the bottom of a valley, surrounded by nature. He agreed to build a small hotel for tourists.

A New Chinese Style of Architecture

Pei wanted to help the Chinese people use a **style** of **architecture** that they liked better than the ordinary block buildings they had. Pei traveled to Suzhou to visit the home where his grandfather used to live. Pei decided that most Chinese appreciated gardens and nature. It was a **traditional** part of Chinese **culture**.

Pei **designed** the hotel to save as many trees as he could. Two

Pei designed indoor gardens when he built the Fragrant Hill Hotel in China.

of the trees in the garden were 800 years old. He used different shaped windows to frame the gardens outside. Pei found unique stones to decorate the ponds in the gardens. The stones were 20 feet (6 meters) tall and worn by weather into unusual forms. The garden paths were made with different colored pebbles from a stream near the Chinese border with Vietnam.

Pei soon discovered that construction was very difficult in China. A similar building in the United States might have 200 workers. At Fragrant Hill more than 3,000 workers were needed because they did not have enough bulldozers and cranes.

President Reagan presented Pei with the Pritzker Architecture Prize in 1983.

Pei later talked about the project as the most difficult of his life. He hoped to make a uniquely Chinese building, but the government officials were expecting a **modern** building. When the hotel opened in 1982, the Americans found it beautiful. The Chinese thought it looked ordinary. One official said it looked too Chinese.

The Pritzker Architecture Prize

The following year Pei received the Pritzker **Architecture** Prize. This award is given to one architect each year. It is the highest honor for architects. Pei received $100,000 with his prize.

He used the money to set up a **scholarship** for Chinese architecture students to study in the United States. To win the scholarship, the students had to promise to return to China after their studies. Pei wanted the students to use their education to help China, just as he once hoped to do.

Bank of China Tower in Hong Kong

Though some Chinese did not like Pei's Fragrant Hill Hotel, government officials asked him in 1982 to **design** a **skyscraper** for the Bank of China in Hong Kong. His father had worked for the Bank of China when he lived there. Pei decided he wanted to take the project. He felt his father would be proud.

The bank would be a big challenge. The **site** was very small, so the building would need to be tall. Because Hong Kong has typhoons, the building needed to be strong enough to stand up in the wind. Pei designed a frame that would stand up to strong winds. This design was easier to build than the **traditional** rectangle shape of most skyscrapers.

When the Bank of China Tower opened in 1989, it was the tallest building in Asia. It is 70 stories tall. The design is stepped so that the tallest tower points upward at the top. It was the tallest building Pei ever built, and in many ways, the most successful. Everyone liked it.

The 70-story Bank of China in Hong Kong is the tallest building Pei designed.

Tiananmen Square Tragedy

In 1989 several thousand Chinese students gathered in Tiananmen Square in Beijing to honor a leader who had died. Tiananmen Square is a large public **plaza** in front of the **Forbidden City** in Beijing. As the crowd of students grew over the next few weeks, they began to speak of freedom and their right to speak out against the government. A newspaper reported that the student protests were against the law. The following day hundreds of thousands of students and workers met in Tiananmen Square. The protesters demanded to speak to the government leaders. Some protesters carried signs that said they wanted **democracy**, not **communism**. Thousands camped out in the Square.

The government of China did not allow students and citizens to speak freely. China's leaders worried as the protests spread to other cities around the country. They feared a **rebellion** might force a change in government. The President of China sent the army to clear the Square. But so many students blocked the streets that the army could not get near Tiananmen Square.

Late one night in early June, the army came back. This time they had tanks and many soldiers. They drove their tanks down crowded streets. Some protesters were crushed under the tanks. Soldiers began firing machine guns into the huge crowd. Most protesters ran away, but some fought back with rocks. The fighting went on all night long. The next morning, Tiananmen Square was empty. No one knows how many people died that night.

Pei was horrified at the killings. Before the events he believed China was moving toward a more democratic government. He wrote an article in the *New York Times* that expressed his sadness at the deaths. In 1989 his work on the Bank of China in Hong Kong was not finished.

Pei used a glass pyramid to mark the new entrance to the Louvre Museum in Paris.

Chapter 6:
The Grand Louvre Project

With so much success, there seemed to be no challenge that Pei had not met. Then, in 1983, French President Francois Mitterrand asked Pei to think about a plan to **modernize** the Louvre Museum in Paris. The Louvre had once been the palace of eleven French kings. For almost 200 years it had served as a museum. No other building in Paris meant as much to the French people.

Pei asked Mitterrand for time to study the Louvre. He did not want to accept the project if he could not solve the problems in a beautiful way. The Louvre was not **designed** as a museum, and most visitors had to ask where to find the main entrance. There was also little room for the storage of art. Pei learned that there was only enough room to **display** ten percent of the thousands of art objects the Louvre owned. Most visitors came to see the painting *Mona Lisa*, but then left.

Pei read books about French history and **architecture**. He walked along the streets of Paris and studied the **courtyards** of the Louvre. He knew that nothing he added would blend with the old building. Pei did not want to change the building itself. But he knew that he could make improvements. He decided that the building needed a new entrance and at least two underground levels for new **displays** and storage. By building underground, he would preserve the historic building.

The Battle of the Pyramid

Pei began to plan the entrance first. He built a wooden model of the Louvre and tried different ideas in the courtyard. If he used a solid shape, it would block the view of the building. He decided that the entrance should be made of glass. This would allow visitors to look through it, and it would reflect the sky. He wanted the entrance to be large enough to welcome large crowds. A **pyramid** allowed him enough space to create a large courtyard below ground.

Mitterrand liked the idea of a pyramid right away. But many French people hated the idea of a modern glass structure in front of their historic treasure. Newspaper writers wrote that the project should stop. Government officials told Pei that pyramids were used for the dead, like in Egypt. Pei explained that pyramid shapes were used by every **culture**, including France. He stayed calm and continued planning the underground space.

At first, many people did not like the idea of a pyramid next to the historic museum.

In 1985, Pei used a crane to set up four wires in the shape of the planned pyramid. For four days more than 60,000 people came to look at the size of the pyramid. Pei promised the glass would be clear, so the size and impact would be similar to the model they saw. The French realized that Pei's pyramid was not as large as they feared. The project moved ahead.

The Underground Improvements

Below the **pyramid** Pei **designed** tunnels that went to the three different wings of the museum. Visitors entered through the pyramid and took **escalators** down one level. There they bought tickets, and took the tunnel that led to the art they wanted to see. One tunnel was lined with restaurants and shops. Other tunnels allowed museum workers to move art from one wing to another. In the past, they often lowered large pieces out of the windows to move them to another wing.

When the entrance and underground space opened in 1989, Pei called it the greatest challenge of his career. The new **courtyard** between the wings of the old museum had the pyramid at the center. Smaller pyramids let sunlight into the underground tunnels. A large pool reflected the pyramid and the older museum. For all the successful projects Pei built in his life, this one gave him the most satisfaction. It was a success both in beauty and in the way it attracted new visitors to Paris's greatest art museum.

The Grand Louvre Project Part II

When the pyramid opened in 1989, the Great Louvre project was only half done. The pyramid solved the problem of a new entrance to the museum. The underground levels organized the way visitors entered the different areas in the three wings. The lowest level gave the museum storage space. But to get more space to **display** art, the north wing of the building would have to be modified.

People enter the Louvre Museum by taking a spiral staircase down to a lobby beneath the glass pyramid.

Pei added skylights to the upper floors.

The north wing of the Louvre had been used for government offices. Three open **courtyards** in the wing were used for parking. When the officials moved out in 1989, Pei went to work on this new project. First he dug out the gravel parking lots in the courtyards. He added glass roofs above them. These new courtyards became homes for large sculptures.

Pei covered the north wing with a glass dome. This allowed the museum to display large statues in the protected courtyard.

The great staircases and old courtyard walls were saved. The new rooms around the courtyards doubled the **display** space in the Louvre. More than 4,000 works of art that had been in storage were now on display. Pei had solved all of the problems facing the old museum. Now more people visited the Louvre, and they stayed longer. The grand opening was held on November 18, 1993. This date was exactly 200 years after the Louvre first became a public museum.

Pei also used a pyramid for the entrance to the Rock and Roll Hall of Fame and Museum, in Cleveland, Ohio.

Chapter 7:
Pei's Place in History

By 1990 Pei was tired of working so much. He was 72 years old and he wanted to spend more time in his garden and with Eileen. He turned the daily management work of his company over to others. He planned to continue working, just not on the huge projects of his past. However Pei did not wait long to take on new projects, and some were quite large.

The Rock and Roll Hall of Fame and Museum

Before Pei left his company, he agreed to **design** the Rock and Roll Hall of Fame and Museum in Cleveland, Ohio. He did not know much about rock and roll, but his children helped persuade him. He traveled to Graceland to learn about Elvis Presley. He listened to records by the Beatles, Elvis Presley, and Bob Dylan. To everyone's surprise, Pei accepted the project.

Pei believed that rock and roll and **modern architecture** were both about energy. He **designed** a very modern building on the shoreline of Lake Erie. Pei used a glass triangle around the entrance. When the building opened in 1995, many famous rock and roll musicians such as Chuck Berry, Jerry Lee Lewis, and Bruce Springsteen played a concert.

Pei's Sons Start Their Own Company

For more than 15 years, Pei's sons Chien Chung and Sandi had worked in his company. They worked on important projects with their father, such as the Louvre and the Bank of China in Hong Kong. In 1992 the brothers started their own company called Pei Partnership Architects. While Pei took on smaller projects, his sons went after large ones.

In 1994 Pei and his sons were chosen to design the Bank of China Headquarters in downtown Beijing, China. Pei's sons did all the traveling and the management, but they asked their father to help with the design. The building opened in 2001, and this time, the Chinese liked it.

In many ways Pei's sons have learned from their father. An eleven-story **courtyard** welcomes visitors to the bank. The courtyard has a goldfish pond with huge stones, just like the ones at Fragrant Hill Hotel. Chien Chung and Sandi selected the stones from the same park 1,800 miles (2,900 km) away, and had them

The Bank of China headquarters is in the heart of Beijing's financial district.

sent to Beijing by train. The courtyard garden is so popular, bank officials allow visitors to come in and enjoy the garden along with their bank workers.

Back to Suzhou

With the success of the bank in Beijing, Pei and his sons accepted an opportunity to **design** a museum in Suzhou. In the city of his ancestors, Pei designed a museum for artwork that is thousands of years old. The museum has space for tearooms, a library, a study center, and gardens. The **design** combines the Chinese **style** of **architecture** Pei loved in his grandfather's Suzhou home with the modern style he knows so well.

Pei's buildings show he values quality in building materials and in details. Every building looks as though it belongs there. This comes from Pei's determination to find just the right kind of design for each project. Perhaps most important, Pei designs buildings with the people that will use them in mind. He wants them to use his buildings, **courtyards**, and gardens.

His Highest Honor

Over his lifetime, Pei has won hundreds of architecture awards and medals. In 1992, President George H. W. Bush gave him the Medal of Freedom, the highest achievement award given by the United States government. However, for Pei, the most important award he received was the Medal of Liberty in 1986. President Ronald Reagan gave this special award to twelve immigrants who had become American citizens. The medal was presented at the ceremony to celebrate the **restoration** of the Statue of Liberty. With the Medal of Liberty, Pei knew he had become an American, but he never forgot his Chinese **traditions**.

These people each won the Medal of Liberty in 1986. Pei is third from left.

Glossary

allies friendly countries that help each other during war

architecture activity of designing buildings or the style of design used for buildings. Someone who designs and plans new buildings is called an architect.

civil war war between different groups of people in the same country

colony part of one country that is controlled by another country

communism system of government where all property is owned by the government, and all people have an equal share of the land and businesses. A follower of communism is a communist.

courtyard open space in the center of a building

culture stage, form, or kind of civilization

design draw or think up something new that can be built or made. A plan, model, or sketch for something that can be built or made is known as a design.

democracy system of government where the people choose their leaders

develop to plan new housing, shops, or offices for a piece of land

display to show artwork in a special room or location. When artwork or something else is shown somewhere, that showing is known as a display.

engineering science in which natural energy and properties of matter are used to construct things that are useful to humans, such as structures, machines, and products

escalator moving stairway

Forbidden City ancient palace grounds of the former emperors of China

missionary person sent somewhere to spread a religious faith

modern architecture new style of architecture that began in the 1930s

modernize to change a building to bring it up-to-date

plaza open area that often has trees, walkways, and places to sit down

pyramid structure that has a square as its base and four triangular sides that meet at a point

real estate land and the buildings that are on it, often used when selling or buying property

rebel someone who fights against his country's government

restoration to bring a building or monument back to its original condition

scholarship money given to a student to pay for education

skyscraper very tall building

site construction place where a specific building will be built

style individual way of doing things or designing

tradition handing down of information, beliefs, or customs from one generation to the next

warlord someone who rules other people with force and weapons

Timeline

1917	Ieoh Ming Pei was born on April 26 in Guangzhou, China.
1918	Pei's family moves to Hong Kong to escape the warlords.
1927	Pei's family moves to Shanghai when his father is promoted.
1930	Pei's mother dies.
1935	Pei travels to the United States to study architecture.
1940	Pei graduates from MIT with a bachelor of architecture degree.
1942	Pei marries Eileen Loo.
1945	Pei's first son, T'ing Chung, Is born.
1946	Pei graduates from Harvard with a master of architecture degree.
1945	Pei's second son, Chien Chung, is born.
1950	Sandi, Pei's third son is born.
1952	Builds a country home in Katonah, New York.
1955	Eileen and Pei become American citizens on November 11.
1956	Mile High Center opens.
1960	Creates his own company, I.M. Pei & Associates; Daughter Liane is born.
1967	National Center for Atmospheric Research opens.
1978	East Building of the National Gallery of Art opens.
1979	John F. Kennedy Library opens.
1982	Fragrant Hill Hotel opens.
1983	Wins the Pritzker Architecture Prize.
1986	Pei given the Medal of Liberty by President Ronald Reagan.
1989	Bank of China Tower in Hong Kong opens.
1992	Pei given the Medal of Freedom by President George H. W. Bush.
1993	The Grand Louvre Project I and II opens.
1995	Rock and Roll Hall of Fame opens.
2001	Bank of China headquarters in Beijing opens.

Further Information

Further Reading

Boyer Binns, Tristan. *Chinese Americans*. Chicago: Heinemann Library, 2003.

Milo, Francesco. *The Story of Architecture*. New York: Peter Bedrick Books, 2001.

Raatma, Lucia. *Chinese Americans*. Chanhassen, MN: Child's World, 2002.

Severance, John B. *Skyscrapers: How America Grew Up*. New York: Holiday House, 2000.

Weaver, Janice. *Building America*. Toronto: Tundra Books, 2002.

Addresses

Archicenter: Chicago Architecture Foundation
224 S. Michigan Avenue
Chicago, IL 60604

**Architecture in Education Program
AIA Philadelphia Chapter**
117 S. 17th Street
Philadelphia, PA 19103

**Chinese Historical Society
of America**
650 Commercial Street
San Francisco, CA 94133

**Museum of Chinese in the
Americas (MoCA)**
70 Mulberry Street, Second Floor
New York, NY 94133

Organization of Chinese Americans
1001 Connecticut Avenue N.W.,
Suite 601
Washington, DC 20036

**Pei Cobb Freed & Partners
Architects LLP**
88 Pine Street
New York, NY 10005 USA

Index